TARA BERGIN was born and grew up in Dublin. She moved to
En~~gland~~ in 2002. In 2012 ~~she completed her PhD research at~~
N~~ewcastle University.~~

TARA BERGIN

This is Yarrow

CARCANET

First published in Great Britain in 2013 by
Carcanet Press Limited
Alliance House
Cross Street
Manchester M2 7AQ

www.carcanet.co.uk

A CIP catalogue record for this book is available from the British Library

ISBN 978 1 84777 236 7

The publisher acknowledges financial assistance from Arts Council England

Typeset by XL Publishing Services, Exmouth
Printed and bound in England by SRP Ltd, Exeter

I am at war with myself, it's true, you have no idea how much, beyond anything you may guess, and I say contradictory things which are […] in real tension with one another, and which make me what I am, are my life's blood, and will be the death of me.

— Jacques Derrida

The glamour
Of childish days is upon me, my manhood is cast
Down in the flood of remembrance, I weep like a child for
the past.

— D.H. Lawrence

For my husband and my son

Contents

Looking at Lucy's Painting of the Thames at Low Tide Without Lucy Present

Water is terribly difficult to paint –
and to drink, also, don't you find? – it's terribly difficult
to drink water. In winter in particular.
Lucy says we must drink eight glasses a day,
but the truth is I can't abide it.

Lucy's face looks terribly bruised, do you find?
Especially under artificial light.
Is everything all right with Lucy, do you think?
She seems quite abstracted, most of the time –

and artists *will insist* on painting water,
despite its obvious difficulty
and, above all, its secrecy
(they say the marine world is notoriously 'close-knit').

I detest it, of course – the work.
I simply can't stand the academic realism of the whole endeavour.
That's not to say it isn't worth something.

On the contrary.

Acting School

Tomorrow is the day of the main performance:
I play, not by choice, a spritely, foul-mouthed American.
Generally, the cast is following the *Strasberg Method*:
we never try to be jealous, or stirred up for no reason at all.
In today's rehearsal we begin, as always,
with articulation:

Lips: trill
Jaw: spring
Palate: soft
Tongue: pointing
pointing out from the mouth and we are humming all the while,

humming all the time
and all the time centring –
rubbing the centre
and rocking and aligning:
pulling the string up from the crown and not the chin
and looking out with the eyes not the chin
and before speaking,
before singing,
all the time increasing
our capacity for breath.

The Director has told us that exiting well is an art.
It will prove no less vital to your life as an artist,
he says,
than entering.
While the good entrance might be slightly more central,
exiting well could be a turning point in your career.

And now we must practise how to drink water
when there is no water.
Once Aoife ceases to argue
about the fact that we have nothing in our mouths,
we can get on with the task of learning.
Swallowing air, as the Director says,

might not be the same as swallowing water,
but for our purposes at least,
there is a sufficient amount of physical truth
in what we do.

Water is Difficult

Oxygen and hydrogen in liquid state,
convertible by heat into steam,
and by cold into ice
(Mr. H. Fowler, Mr. F. Fowler,
you do make things sound nice).
In summary: water is a liquid consisting chiefly of this.
Just one of these things, so the Fowlers say,
is due to appetite.
But I have a thirst /
I have a fear of / I have a sin of –
and Lucy is on her knees before you, water,
admitting that she might not believe.
'What does it do, what does it do?'
she asks, 'except *leave?*'

Tell her before she herself decides to go:
Things break – even water.
Water must break
if we are to enter and live.

All Fools' Day: An Academic Farewell

No negotiation.
No negotiation before departure.

In this paper
I will make no direct reference to the above title,
or expand on the possible relevance of my argument,
symbolic or otherwise,
to the main topic.

I will go on to plagiarise
several well-known poets and writers
without citing their work
or acknowledging their influence on my thoughts in any way.
See, for example, the epigraph to this abstract,
a quote which was taken from the leader of the opposition in
Cairo (2011)
yet used here out of context in an entirely inappropriate setting.

Finally, I will put to myself the same questions
that my examiners –
so I have been warned –
will put to me.

Each of my answers
will be indirect,
unsuitable,
and ultimately unclear.
I shall fail, in other words, to satisfy the criteria
set by the examiners and their governing board.

Don't ask who's keeping house –
no one's keeping house today.

Questions

1. Did you ever play the piano again after your mother died and if so, what did you play?

2. Could you sing and did you ever sing later on in life when you were married and living away from Moscow?

3. If you can remember (and please try) what songs exactly did you sing?

4. What did you think when you took your pen in your hand and wrote that letter to Stalin?

5. Did you feel a kind of heat of the mind and also a chill somewhere in your stomach?

6. Did your hand shake?

7. Is time mostly to do with feeling and thought?

8. Is time a trap, in your opinion?

9. Am I completely responsible for what I do with time, or not at all, or partly?

10. How powerful – would you say – is a poem not to do with war?

11. Did you like the violin?

12. Were you an insomniac?

13. Compared, I mean, to one about war?

You Could Show a Horse

(an experiment in collage)

You could show a horse, *you might see some riderless horse*,
galloping among the *rushing among the enemy* with its mane in the
wind *with his mane flying in the wind* causing heavy casualties *and
doing no little mischief with his heels*. Or you could show a man,
mutilated, *some maimed warrior may be seen* lying on the ground
fallen to the earth shielding himself in some way *covering himself with
his shield* with his enemy bent over him and trying to *while the enemy
bending over him tries to deal him a deathstroke* – or show a lot of
people fallen on to a dead horse *A number of men fallen in a heap
over a dead horse* – and you could show the men *you would see
some of the victors*, leaving the fight, *abandoning the conflict* emerging
from the *and issuing from the crowd* using both hands *rubbing their
eyes and cheeks with both hands*, to clean their faces, *to clean them of
the dirt made by their watering eyes* now coated *smarting from the
dust and smoke* in tears which have poured from their dust-filled
eyes.

Himalayan Balsam for a Soldier

They don't see me but I walk
into Fitzgeralds with them the half-wounded,
I sit in there at the high table with my pint,
half-wounded, thinking, I will drag my
wounds in here.
I drag myself in and up to the high stool
among the guys with one arm and they
don't see me.
Here is your talisman I say, I whisper
hold it in your good hand and sing one
of your songs for me.
How does it go? Oh how does it go again?
There is blood on my hand, la la,
there is blood on my hand, la, la.
Your talisman, I say, a foul flower.
Hold it in your hand and how full your good
hand will be with the
exploding.

Dancing

All the branches of the plum tree
are in flower and you are dancing
in your sleep.
Serbia is in your hair.
It is a white flower.
It is your right foot.

Serbia's arm is young
around your waist.

All the flowers are gone.
The plum tree's branches
are bent with weight.

Sonnets for Tracey

i. Permission to Fire

Oh Tracey you have pre-empted me –
You know I feel you do it with my tongue in your cheek,
Rob me of my weakness and my tricks.
Yes, we can open our soft white thighs,
But everyone is so deeply *chauvinistic*
Don't you think?
Even we are, with our naivety.
You with your misspelt words,
And your off-kilter eye,
Like a wall-eye on a sick horse,
Me with my envy and my Capitals,
My longing to lie down on your rags.

I can see that in all this trickery we are the same.
Oh Tracey we should be ashamed.

ii. Handbook

It's easy to handle girls once you've been introduced to them,
but this one's hard, with her sweet physique,
always wiping her face, always wiping and pushing at her lovely cheeks.
Her left hand seems trapped, but her right hand is free –
What will I say to this one, Tracey?

Last night I saw my lover
in the agony of death.
First she fell on her knees and then onto me.
I picked her up and wrapped her in a sheet.
She was as light as an empty box might be.
I checked my Dictionary of Dreams:
I will have improper thoughts,
or do improper deeds.

Come over and talk to me.

iii. X Prostitutism

'The fat bud of the peony is a whore if I am —
we can see her on her back, plump and ready to open,
and I could paint her torn-open bloom, posed out in the open,
but I am not a peony-painter and I am
not a rich fat whore like the peony:
I am a poor girl from a poor town.

I was a young girl in a young town
when I dreamt that I was stung.
The red and swollen bud of my thumb
throbbed with false pain all morning.
I mixed a poultice and put it on,
and my thumb turned white with kaolin.

I am a dirty girl in a dirty town,
but men prefer me.'

iv. Tambour Café, Marienstr. 16

Tracey sat without a soul in sight,
without a soul looking in, as if she had no light
on inside, as if she herself had not been in the café
but perhaps sitting in the theatre nearby,
privately performing in her seat.
The waitress wore neat shoes and a short skirt —
such a strange combination but alluring almost.
If it weren't for the loneliness pinning her in,
Tracey might have asked her back — asked her to lift
her chin, while balancing the tray on her hip.
Tracey pouted her lips,
then didn't know what to do.

Awkward and vain she sat at the black–green glass,
while the small crowd laughed, over in the *Theater-Kasse*.

Composition for the Left Hand

Last night I met a trophy hunter
who admired my slender fingers –
he held my left hand up to the light
and praised the pretty white skin
on my palm and let me flare my fingers
out like the antlers of a stag – he took my wrist
and I didn't insist on a phone number –
I gave him mine,
even knowing what his game was.
I played it and all the time I knew
he'd want to claim some trophy or some prize.
He was a trophy hunter –
believe me, he had guns
in a glass cabinet like the one
my grandmother kept her champagne glasses in
(such rich families I've been involved in)
and he cleaned them regularly
with a long thin pipe
and a soft oily rag –
he was a paying hunter, you see,
the best in the country,
and he really didn't want me at all.
He only wanted some kind of trophy,
something pale and palmate
that he could hang on his wall
after the whole ugly thing was over.

Christmas Window, Armistice Day

What a shame he chose that day to come to town –
a mistake, of course – his timing was bad –
but how awful it should happen just as he passed –
just as he was passing the ridiculous toys and
the overwhelming noise of the Christmas music –
that he should choose that day and that time to pass!
Eleven o'clock! so that when they shut the music off
for two whole minutes
and turned off the movement of the toys
for two whole minutes,
and all the light and the noise
turned off from inside the huge window,
the silence and the stillness
that he found himself looking in at
was most marked, and most terrifying.
The stilled elves with their open jaws
and upraised hands –
how cruel their little bodies had become,
how wooden, like men who die,
their stiff jaws unhinged
and their hammers like little guns,
paused and false-seeming.

Was it a mistake?

Was what a mistake? We don't know –
the two minutes finished and the stiff,
shot-off little jaws started to sing once more.
Down came the hammers he'd mistaken for guns,
up came the arms he'd mistaken for arms.
Oh gaudy, gaudy little things,
the foolishly mouthing jaws never meeting the song,
always off-kilter, always getting their timing wrong.

And what had he done?
And what was he going to do now?

We don't know.

Sonnet for Catherine Who Never Turned Up

That night after class I dreamt of you, Catherine Mooney –
at home and unable to come –
I had you forgetful and
wearing fingerless gloves,
writing a sonnet with couplets
that didn't sound like couplets,
and one of the best villanelles
in the English tongue.

Brave Catherine.
Don't be afraid to stay away –
sometimes it's all that can be done.
Our secretary rings and rings
your unplugged phone,
while the envious ones push on.

Military School

The analysis of battle begins here at our desks.
The voice of violence enters our mouths
and our skin, and under my own nails
I hear it seduce me. I argue with nothing it says.
The voice is a swan of the estuary.
It laments, it recites:
Sixteen Dead Men; The Rose Tree,
out of pages yellowed from 1953 –
it bangs oh it bangs
a bodhran.
I agree.
I denounce my motherland,
propose fidelity to my fatherland.
It begins here,
the voice of beauty begins here,
lovely out of the desk.
We mark our youth on the
photocopied maps with black crosses,
obediently we mark our youth.

White Crow

Come here little white crow,
let me stroke your soft fur.
Let me take your white fur
and wear it as a long coat.
I will wear it for my wedding day.
I will make vows in the fire station
where bells like sirens deafen:
they will warn of burning,
on that day of our wedding,
and on the hour of our wedding
for every year after that.

I am unwell, little crow,
I am unwell and far from home
where longing lives in my house.

The Undertaker's Tale of the Notebook
Measuring 1 x 2 cm

For forty years I have had in my possession:
A notebook, morocco-bound and blue in colour
which was so small it could be covered over by a thumb.
I found it at the bottom of her
apron pocket;

And for forty years I have had in my throat
the rotten apple of Mordovia
which for forty years
I could not swallow;

And I have held in my possession
the year Nineteen-Forty-
One:
a year too small for her
to write in.

Rapeseed

He thought my clothes were my skin.
He thought these soft things,
this lace and these buttons,
were things I belonged in,
but I do not belong in them.
I told him but he didn't see.

Look, he went on stroking my gloves
and my things,
thinking, what fine skin – Oh
Mister My, My –
I did take thee and thou me.
And after the ceremony?
Quiet, quiet.

We drove past rapeseed.
Fields of it through the window
on the full hot air – oh sweet,
oh stale, oh clinging to the air –
oh shame, oh full, oh cruel.

How we feared its fierceness!
How we worried it would overlook us!
We feared too much,
thinking the world
is reached only in violence.

Red Flag

Once one of them showed me how to:
You turn this (the right) hand to grasp the stock.
You turn this (the left) hand to grasp the barrel.
He touched my knee,
and I hid my surprise –
but now he's changed his tune.

36, 37, 38.9

I've a fever little sparrow, I am sick.
Their flag is flying red,
I can hear it from my window,
I hear it tattered like a torn red rag.
Go and get it little bird,
go and tell them danger! danger!

I will wear it as my Sunday Dress.
I'll wear it walking on the moor
where they practise with their guns.

38.9, 37, 36

How ashamed they'll be
to hurt a young and pretty
girl like me.

The Passion Flower

I don't drink in front of the barman.
I don't shake his hand or lift the drink
to my mouth while he is watching,
for fear he will exclaim at the sight
of my hands.
How red, he will say,
how almost black with the cold.
He thinks me rude but it's the
muteness in my hands.

When he has looked away
I take my glass and my change
to the small dark table.
I hear the big voices, pointing away
from thought, to speaking,
but I cannot talk.
I sit in the corner with my clenched
tongue and my tight, swollen hands.
I sit and I think of the single ringlet
and the green star of leaves.

I think of the meaning found for these things.

That the leaves are the clutching hands of soldiers,
that the tendrils are the whips –
that the five sepals and five petals are ten disciples,
that the five stamens are the wounds.

That's what they say it represents.

The Sick Child, at the Time of the Diamond Jubilee

Yesterday they did something
which was deceitful in the marketplace.
Today they are hanging up flags.
Stringing up colours on their bright village greens –
and it will be all so pretty for you to see;
and it will be all so pretty to me.

And the cows have calved,
and the sheep have lambed,
and the May Flower has flowered
on the May Tree.
And it blushes so sweetly for us to see;
and it blushes so sweetly for me.

But worse is to come.
God will make the decision about a
man's position, and will become, once again,
politically implicated.
Oh poor Pop in the heavens, O Lord. Oh my.
What a long weekend we are having,
you and I.

And what did we do?
Rubbed calamine on the tiniest back in the isle,
a neat little back, all rough and red and lumpy.
How he twisted in his bed.
How he didn't sleep.
How we missed so suddenly
(as though it had only just been lost)
the way things used to be.

Restriction

There has been this feeling,
of restriction.
In the hands especially –
So much so
I think of them as bandaged.
I think of them as motionless,
polite,
and resting on the table,
at a distance, as it were.
And all this time I am busy.
I call up whole boats,
whole fish, whole houses,
but they get added to a list
of things to do
when I can use my hands.
I get breathless climbing,
thinking up whole men,
whole women, and I
add them to the list.
I get breathless standing:
whole hawthorns, whole ash trees,
and I add these also.
I try to understand
why I feel this way,
why I have this feeling
of restriction in the hands.
I dream of my hands:
they shock me with what they do.
I try to understand
why I dream these things.
I call up a whole future.
I add it to the list.

Bridal Song

The melting ice gave me a sign in winter,
it dripped on my head and
you know, you know, it said.
Then in the spring the bird–cherry tree gave me:
a bridal bough,
and said again: *you know.*

Only the blackbird in the summer won't speak.
I think he is ignoring me.
He just sits in his seat
and whistles a merry tune, which goes:

Hold out your palms, young Mary,
Hang your head, young bride-to-be,
Set your heart on sorrow for
You never listened to me.

The Confession

It was my fault for kneeling in your dark chamber or closet
when I told you my name was –
dee da, dee da
it was my fault that I knelt in your cell that day,
yes it was mine when I put your fingers to my forehead
and said cross me like I am the Trinity,
and bowed for you to put the Rosary on me
and it was mine, it was mine!
Because thrilling your humming alarmed me.
And your humming was –
dee da dee da
and your humming was –
dee da, de dum
and it was my fault.
But your eyes were as bright as a blind bird's
and your heart beat like the heart of a swift
that is trapped
or a trapped swift that is dying
when you said Rosemary,
Oh Rose –
dee da, da dee.

Glinka

Look at little Mikhail Ivanovich:

> five flights up in his grandmother's room,
> wrapped in furs, and perched like a pianist
> on her padded, crocheted, dressing-table stool –

Porter! Grandmother calls.
Keep the thermostat at twenty-five degrees –

> Mikhail eats sweets,
> wrapped and stuffy in his furs.
> On Sunday he hears the sound of the street:
> a choir, five flights down.

Meeka, Meeka,
come away from the window.

> Grandmother wrings her hands.
> The village church rings her bell.
> Young Mikhail knows all is well.

The Pressed Iris

How neat my little flower will be,
pressed hard within its flower-press.
But I dare not twist apart the screws
and take apart the wooden box.

I cut you know I cut my finger
on the leaf, and said 'I dare not look.'
And now the same – I dare not look:
my showy flowers; my swords…

no longer weapons.

Oh poor little swords,
poor, poor little flower
that I cannot see.

Pilinszky at the Tenshi no Tobira

Come to Mii-Chan,
put your vulnerable face on my knee.
Try to remember
(let the sirens lull you back) –
tell me how they called you up.
Only *nineteen*? Shame on them.

Come to Chan-Lii,
put your vain head on my lap
and – if you can tell me –
what exactly did you *do*?

Oh little Jancsi, come to Su-li,
are your hands so red?
Is there dirt on your hands, Jancsi,
now that they are dead?

Come and lie your paper-head
on Mii-Chan's knee.
Let my tiny bamboo hook you
into thinking you are loved.

You said you would lie down full length,
Jancsi.
You said you would be obedient and good.

Ask for one of us by name, Jancsi-Chan
(for 500 extra Yen),
we too are only nineteen, maybe less.

Swiss Station Room

Dear Anne, what a show –
my tongue was going
like the red second-hand
on that clock, on that clock
at the station, did you see it?
When he watched me –
Did you see how my cheeks
were flushed – how my cheeks were hot?
Did you see how my hands on my lap
pulled and twisted at my dress –
Could he see? How shy?
I spoke vainly: it was false.

Liebe Anne, you spoke so much better,
like a man, like a bull –

Ay ay ay –
it's becoming
it's becoming habitual
and I…

How vain the sea is also, though,
have you noticed?
Gazing forever in the glass,
always avoiding, avoiding us both.

St Patrick's Day Address, 1920

I clutch a bunch of wood sorrel in my fist,
unsure whether to pin it on;
I haven't long, the 3 leaves will close down at night.
But how we flatter, how we coax –
even though we know it is a useless gift.
Still we insist on bending backwards
to touch the filthy stone with our lips.
What tradition is this?
Shouldn't we be more careful
who we ask to be our allies?
Shouldn't we be more careful
who we lean out to kiss?

Photograph of Thérèse of Lisieux Holding Lilies

This: a neatly-fitting hood,
like a cap on a bird,
tied beneath her chin,
like Little Red Riding Hood,

and her neck: wrapped up neatly
in the high white cloth,
like a white-throated bird –

and Theresa:
how long you seem to be taking!
Standing there, cradling the lilies,
so white and pretty,
as if you had all the time in the world.

Luckily, they will be patient, the faithful.
They will wait gracefully at the doors of the church,
for the bones of the watchmaker's daughter.

Then they will file up the aisle, all together,
as quiet and excited as brides.

Jack-go-to-bed-at-noon

in memoriam

It is unfair to thieve so cruelly, and in such hot light.
The theft has turned the upper fields white:
they are in shock, and pale from all their downy clocks.
But where is the boy's breath?
How will he blow these candles out?
Goodnight, goodnight, even though it is day;
the flower-head has closed, and turned away.

Studying the Fresco of St Nikolai of Myra

It is the shadow playing havoc
with the blondeness of your hair
because it looks black,
and Marina on your black hair
is a light from the window,
making me sure you're wearing
the Virgin's crown.
Whatever you see,
you know the dying are not guilty.

Through the window the soldiers are marching
and singing, they are singing it is your name-day

Marina, Marina,

and the Church of the Protection of the
Veil stands near your house –
and there is singing in the church,
even if there is no God.

At the Garage

Ask me:
have I fallen in love with the mechanic?
Perhaps – perhaps, for a moment.
He doesn't know what it is.
It's his hands –
so thickly black with engine oil,
so hard-working, and in such high demand.

Ask me:
is there violence in the dirt?
Perhaps – perhaps, for a moment.
Like a criminal's thumb which gets
held firmly by the prison officer
and is then rolled hard onto gummed paper
so that we know, we know, that he is done for –

and even the backs of the mechanic's hands,
as well as the palms, are all inked black,
and everything they touch will be evidence of him –
the keys, the white receipt, my own hand
or cheek
were he to touch it.

Ask me, ask me how that makes me feel!
My cheeks turn pink with the thought of it,
while his blushes, if he had blushed,
would be hidden behind grease –
a soft deep dirt that is soft and thick
like the ink in tins that etchers use.
It makes the whites of his eyes whiter,
and the blues bluer –

Yes, perhaps I am almost in love with the mechanic.
But it is terribly awkward, face to face.
It is terribly awkward to be in such close proximity
to the mechanic, and the dirty girl on the calendar
who is always there, just visible from the small window
where I go afterwards, to pay.

from *The Ballad of Tom Gun*

So there we were, two boys under the eaves,
secretly listening to ourselves and our eager curiosities;
Tom Gun saying things only I believed –
though later he said them again, much more seriously.

And he was a handsome boy, even then,
and he was a clever boy.

But it wasn't until he went away from that city,
and left the prying eyes of the old university,
that he found a place where he could be free
to write down all those things more publicly.

And the old guy at the bathhouse in charge of the locker-keys,
he would say to Tom you wear your heart on your sleeve
you know what that means?
And Tom would say I know what it means.

And Tom would say to him it's what I do.

Ah, but he was just a young boy then.
And I was too.

Training Camp, Whit Monday

The young soldiers sit in a circle on the grass:
they are having a picnic with summer games.

Beyond the group, far off,
two stand together:
one aims
and the other instructs him where to shoot.

A great cracking and clapping from the gun
is carried in the wind to the houses
where a young boy,
who has been taken out to run and play,
stops suddenly at the noises.

What is it, what is it?
(he is a nervous boy) –
and his mother is unsure. What lies
should she tell? What should she say?
What do the other mothers say?
She doesn't know

and so she says:
there's no need to be afraid, off you go and play.
But she has lied, she knows,
and oh she is ashamed.

My Personal Injuries Claim

One wishes one didn't need to
quite as much as one does:

(Do you have a pretty dress?
Do you have a nice pair of shoes?)

Swap, swap, swap.

'He was an artist, judge:
he traced the lines of my face.'

They like that very much.

One, two, three.
How many facets have thee?
Four, five, six.
Too many to fit.
Seven, eight, nine: Judge –
The analyst says it's all in my mind.

There's really nothing wrong –
only sometimes
it pricks one a little.

Garrison Supermarket

No one stands to see – stands to attention –
stands to see – salutes – the soldiers –
no one is red-faced – no one is amazed –
ashamed – no one is afraid –

and their hands are the same –
and their faces are the same –
and no one is afraid –

and even outside, looking in –
as I stand by the odd, jerking machine,
which I put coins in
to keep my child satisfied –

(it moves almost imperceptibly,
but my child doesn't seem to mind)

even then I see no signs –
and even my young child is not at all surprised
to see them dressed for combat
and pacing up and down the aisles.

But then his country is not the same as mine.

At the Lakes with Roberta

Our guide
(with whom Roberta has already been ingratiating herself
in a horribly forward manner)
has taken us to Windermere,
and tomorrow will take us to Grasmere.
Of course I am eager to see,
first-hand, as it were,
the sources of inspiration,
but I fear Roberta's behaviour
shall spoil the entire experience.

Speaking bluntly: she is far too light-hearted;
rather superficial if one may say such a thing,
and she *flatters* him, that's the point,
she flatters him with her incompetence.
I'm afraid I find it unseemly.

The fact is,
if she continues to distract our guide from his duty as guide,
there will be a breach between Roberta and me.
The fault will lie with her:
it's perfectly clear she came only to enjoy The View –
while I can hardly bear it, you see;
I can hardly bear the weight of this poetic air,
the air that WW breathed: such steep atmosphere.
There's nothing for it: one must simply never travel
with one's female companions.

And now, look:
our guide is daring to quote from 'To the Small Celandine'
(never a favourite of mine)
and Roberta's foolish gasps of pleasure hang on the mist.
It's unfortunate, really, that he has been quite so taken in,
so swallowed up by what one might call
a rather ordinary attractiveness.

And clearly I shall remain ignorant for the rest of the tour
about the more – intimate – details
of a poet's life.

Portrait of the Artist's Wife as a Younger Woman

I go to my husband's studio
and I stand looking at her face,
hearing only:
tick-tock, tick-tock.

I stand and I think:
I must measure seven ounces at three.
I must level the scoops with a clean dry knife
(he wanted a wife he wanted a wife) –
I must pick up the baby with its shaking fist,
and go: Shh, shh, little one,
while I sprinkle the milk
like perfume on my wrist,
it's so hot, little one, it's so sour, little thing.

I look at her there.
See where the soft knife's been
at her collarbone and her mouth
which is pink –
like the bark of trees in America,
in the south.

And she doesn't say:
I am free legally to take;
she doesn't say: Shh, shh.
Only I speak.
Only I say: Shh, shh.
Only I say: It's so hot, little one,
it's so sour, little thing.

Stag-Boy

He enters the carriage with a roar –
he clatters in wildly and fills up the carriages with heat,
running through the train, staining the floor
with hooves dirty from the street;
tearing at the ceilings with his new branched horns,
banging his rough sides against the seats and
the women, who try to look away: Gallant!
He sings hard from his throat,
his young belling tearing at his chest,
pushing at his boy-throat.

Stag-boy –

the train's noise hums in his ears,
sharp and high like crickets pulsing
in the tall grass,
and he wounds it with his horns,
maddened like a stung bull,
pushing up his head,
pushing up his mouth for his mother's teat:
Where is her beestings?
Where is the flowered mug she used to warm his milk in?

No good, no good now.

He's smashing out of the train door,
he's banging his hooves in the industrial air,
he's galloping through the city squares,
and drinking from a vandalised spring –

And still his mother walks through the house,
crying: *Stag-boy, oh stag-boy come home!*

If Painting Isn't Over

If painting isn't over
I will say this:
Who have I offended?

1. I have figures that are not figures;
2. I have gone for an undoing of the image.

If painting isn't over
I will admit this:
You have offended your whole life.
You have divided your days.
You have taken your hands
and put them in the drawer.

Queen of the Rodeo

Honey is avoiding all eye contact.
Honey is feeling hemmed in;
is red faced; is experiencing
a rapid beating of the heart.

The judges go wild for Honey.
Honey is the best they'll see for a long time.

Give us a twirl!
calls the crowd
but Honey doesn't twirl –
she can't think of a word to say.
She just opens her mouth
and starts to pray:

O my God, I am heartily sorry
for having offended thee
and I detest my sins above every other evil
because they displease Thee, my God

And what do you know?
The crowd joins in on her act
of contrition –

Flushed in the face with shame,
flushed in the face with anger,
Honey lets the judge drape a sash
over her left breast
and over her shoulder.

The crowd begs Honey for one more prayer,
one more song,
one more anything she has left.
This is they way they mean to go on.

Candidate

1. Can you tell me about yourself?
Many candidates are tripped up by this. Here's an example of what to say: 'I have 10 years of experience in the accounting profession.'

2. What interests you about this job?
Employers seek employees who are enthusiastic about the company. Here's a sample response: 'I've long admired your company's position as a leader in the industry.'

3. What are your weaknesses?
The best approach is to name an actual weakness but follow it up with steps you are taking to overcome the flaw.

4. How many times do a clock's hands overlap in a day?
A question like this can catch you off guard. The interviewer is looking to test your critical thinking skills. Don't be shy when you're figuring out the answer.

5. Do you have any questions?
Use this as an opportunity to show your ability for independent thinking. Don't inquire about salary, benefits, or holidays.

6. Remember: Displaying grace under pressure will highlight your professionalism and help you to stand out as a prospective member of the company.

Feverfew

In the evening when the TV's off
I don't do needlework
and I don't do tapestries
or write cheques to the horticultural society –
I am lacking a sorority, sir.
My curriculum vitae is very poor,
in places –

But really it's no good being vague now.
Here – you must press on my wrist;
you must press on my side.
Is it fast, General Practitioner?
Is it high?
You mustn't send me away for tests, doctor,
we must talk, we must talk about it.

You see, there were five, ten,
maybe twenty of them in a group,
and hanging around;
waiting around like daisies,
only not as good –
not as true –
and what did I do, sir?

I bullied the circle unkindly.
'Up with the traitor!' I cried, in error.
'Down with the star!' And I tore up their union.
I made them fight and become weak,
uprooting them until I smelt their under-smell of death,
and was – too late, too late – horrified.
My continental sister, gasping on the ground,
had hardly cried at all.

And then all that day, doctor, and then all that night,
such heat – and now, still, I feel it radiate!
What do you say about it? What can I take?
Oh, I know I should find out more
before I pull things out –

but I don't.

This is Yarrow

In this country house I had a dream of the city
as if the thick yarrow heads had told me,
as if the chokered dove had told me,
or the yellow elder seeds had made me ask –
and in the dream I went up to the dirty bus station
and I saw the black side of the power station
and as if the brown moth's tapping at the window
made me say it I said, do you still love me?
And when I woke and went to the window,
your tender voice told me: this is yarrow,
this is elder, this is the collared dove.

Notes

The Undertaker's Tale of the Notebook Measuring 1 x 2 cm
Cf. Viktoria Schweitzer, *Tsvetaeva* (Harvill, 1993), p. 375.

Pilinszky at the *Tenshi no Tobira*
Tenshi no Tobira means 'Angel Gateway'. It is the name of a massage parlour in Tokyo, where the young girls specialise in ear-cleaning while dressed as French maids. The phrases 'lie down full length' and 'obedient and good' come from János Pilinszky's 'Under the Winter Sky', trans. János Csokits/Ted Hughes. The line 'what exactly did you *do*?' (spoken here by Chan-Lii) is taken from a letter sent by Ted Hughes to János Csokits in 1974, when Hughes was preparing to write his introductory essay to their Pilinszky translations. Hughes sent a list of questions to Csokits, asking about the reception of Pilinszky's poetry in Hungary and some details about his life. One of his requests was: 'Perhaps you can tell me exactly what he did during the war.' The question was never directly answered at the time, so Hughes ended up writing about it obliquely – causing some reviewers to see his essay as misleading.

Studying the Fresco of St Nikolai of Myra
In her study of the final days of Marina Tsvetaeva, Irma Kudrova tells the story of a ten-year-old boy who went into an empty church in Yelabuga to look at the frescoes. He saw a woman with cropped grey hair squinting, examining the paintings on the walls, and studying the one which showed St Nikolai of Myra restraining the arm of an executioner who had raised his sword over the condemned. The boy said, 'He will save them, they're not guilty of anything.' 'I know that,' the woman answered. The woman was the great Russian poet Marina Tsvetaeva. This event took place only days before Tsvetaeva was found dead, having hanged herself. See Irma Kudrova, *The Death of a Poet* (Overlook Press, 2004).

Stag-Boy
Cf. 'The Boy Changed into a Stag Cries Out at the Gate of Secrets' by Ferenc Júhasz, in various English translations by Ted Hughes, Kenneth McRobbie, Pascale Petit etc. It was during my PhD research into Ted Hughes's translations of the Hungarian poet János Pilinszky that I first came across Hughes's version of Ferenc Júhasz's poem. I was struck by the fact that Hughes had made this version based solely on an English one by Kenneth McRobbie, and began to make a close comparison between his and McRobbie's version, in an attempt to find out what Hughes's alterations told us about his own poetic sensibility. During this work I happened to take

a train to London. A stag party got on at York, and the carriage became, for a short period, territory ruled by them. Their terrible, eager, desperate faces produced in me feelings of interest, pity and fear. That occasion marked a time when as a poet I consciously wished to write about contemporary society. Júhasz's poem, written by a man in 1955 Communist Hungary, altered and conserved through many translations, suddenly appeared to me as a surprising, but wholly fitting model.

Feverfew

The following description of feverfew is given in the Reader's Digest *Field Guide to the Wild Flowers of Britain*: 'It is unlikely that feverfew – almost certainly an introduction from the Continent – would have come to Britain were it not for its value as a medicinal plant. The common name is derived from the Latin *febrifuga*, meaning that the plant was thought to be effective in driving away fevers. The plant had many other uses too, for instance, as a remedy for headaches and as a cure for feminine complaints, especially those connected with childbirth. Once grown commercially as a drug, feverfew is now regarded as no more than a noxious weed to be rooted out, but it is very persistent and hard to eradicate.'

'Down with the star […]' is a reversal of the chorus of 'Rally Round the Flag', an American Civil War protest song ('The Union forever! Hurrah, boys, hurrah! / Down with the traitor, up with the star'). Re-written by Billy Bragg as 'There is Power in a Union'.

Acknowledgements

Thanks to the editors of the following publications, in which some of these poems have appeared: *Best British Poetry 2012* (Salt, 2012), *Lit* (Newcastle University, 2009), *Modern Poetry in Translation*, *New Poetries V* (Carcanet, 2011), *Poetry London*, *PN Review* and *Poetry Review*.